Bulls Bears Dragons on Wall Street

$

Diane Conrad

Bulls Bears & Dragons © 2012
Diane Conrad
Drawings © 2012 Diane Conrad,
Linn Spaulding
Revision © 2018 *Bulls Bears Dragons on Wall Street*

All rights reserved, except in brief quotations embodied in critique or review articles.

Any reproduction, transmission, transfer, import or similar processes in whole or in part, either permanently or temporarily, is against the law.

PhantasmaPress
P.O.Box 1565
Albany, OR 97321, USA
phantasmapress@q.com
phantasmapress.com

More books:
Zen Thunder
Fables of Psyche

Table of Contents

Dedicated..i

Intro..ii

The edge...15

Shhhhhh..16

Resurrection...17

The shadow...18

Old age and death................................19

Time is always......................................20

Bull-Bear-Dragon-steps......................21

Bull rampages......................................23

Bear sleeps...25

Dragon blazes......................................27

Bull Bear Dragon not herd................28

Accountant...29

Accountants sleep...............................30

Can you see..31

How much am I...................................32

Decimals can	33
Money money	34
Money whirls	35
There's more to bubbles	36
There's more to waves	37
Money madness	38
Flip it	39
Powerlust	40
The brilliance	41
Not money	42
Nor	43
Intrepid	44
Scent of success	45
Sparks of success	46
Close the gate	47
Game on	48
At the Exchange	49

Equality Justice 50

Bull Bear Dragon feed 51

The Pit 52

When Bull runs 54

Mystagogue 55

Wizards 56

The swoon 57

Bulls Bears Dragons huff 58

Enough 59

Bull Bear Dragon not quiet 60

Pause 61

The power 62

Bulls Bears Dragons may 63

Drawings

Bull 22

Bear 24

Dragon 26

Emblem 53

Dedicated

To the sharp skill wondrous work
of those who claim their territory on
the Street

To Bulls
ingenious engineers of forward pace

To Bears
vigorous guardians of curb's edge

To their Dragons
the self within
emblazoned Street Warriors

Intro

Bull Bear Dragon
pound the pavement

animal spirits
lick the Street

delicacy
theirs

$$ $$
$ $

The edge   is a promise

LIVE
ON
IT

$$
$

$$
$

Shhhhhhhhhhhhh
let them rise inside you quietly

black Bull
brown Bear
red Dragon

pyrotechnic promises
poised on earth's horizon

$
$$

$
$$

Resurrection
nothing to do with heaven
rather
ashes of aftermath

the Floor is no place for
fallen angels

The shadow
you cast is
your own

meritocracy haunts

Old age and death
promised partners

grave-side meetings
nothing to fear
by those with
eyes open

Time is always
one second ahead of now
speed-strike not fast enough
hesitation for losers

in your pocket carry
the moon crest
click your heels

Bull-Bear-Dragon-steps

dance thunder

stealth courtship afoot

$$ $$
$ $

Bull rampages
risks every step
no matter
landscape

   p
u
      d
     o
    w
     n

$ $
$$ $$

$$
$

$$
$

Bear sleeps late
just enough to
ready for

GAME UP

$
$$

$
$$

Dragon blazes fire
waits

bittersweet shadows
follow

unseen surprises titillate

Bull Bear Dragon
not herd animals
these three

no one
eats
dust

$$ $$
$ $

Accountants
minister unto each
enlighten every path
to a successful ending
let each forget the beginning

gather the bones

$ $
$$ $$

Accountants sleep
in sugared dreams

puffed ledgers
as pillows

$$ $$
$ $

Can you see
in the shadow of
your bank account
a worker's
callous hands?

$ $
$$ $$

$$ $$
$ $

How much is one creature worth?
Let each count the numbers

How worthy is one creature?
Let each count the deeds

Soul calculator!

Decimals can be honorable!?

        Who sits next to God?

Numbers are truth!?

        Accountants?

    Heroes chosen wisely?

    Lodestar?

$$
$

$$
$

Money money
pony up up
you're in
game on

Be the green!   What color truth?

$
$$

$
$$

$$ $$
$ $

Money
whirls between
now and tomorrow
flutters uncontrolled
in emissary wind

catcher catch can

$ $
$$ $$

$$ $$
$ $

There's more to bubbles
than circumference

blow-out power

hold ground

hold breath

$ $
$$ $$

$$ $$
$ $

There's more to waves
than crests

thunder calls
blood rushes

ride on
bubbles

cryptocurrency?

$$ $$

$ $

Money madness

          game of

     lustfun

              buy

gather

                    sell
          influence

                 fox madness

$ 38 $

$$ $$

$$
$

$$
$

Flip it

work both sides

a master's craft

fliptastical

$
$$

$
$$

$$ $$
$ $

Powerlust is
addictive
go for it
never
stop

Hotstuff your eyes are cold

The brilliance of brilliant
the shine of coins
stories of radiance
scintillates cents on nonsense?

Like fireflies
drawn to fire
are you consumed
by flame of fame?

Your life symbolled by
more than your name?

Your luster
blinding children?

$$
$

$$
$

Not
money
but
its glint

Shine on!

Shades on!

$
$$

$
$$

Nor

Bull Bear Dragon

blink

Intrepid blindness when
stomping toward
sundown

life lingers in
the dark

Scent of success
settles
in short sentiment

tomorrow only surmises

$$ $$
$ $

Sparkles of success.
                  .swish like
    runaway trains.
                  .tracks straight
     never ending.
                  .elusive destination
              .
              .
   unparalleled points

Feng Shui ?

$$
$

$$
$

Close the gate

caution is
not the path
of doubt

word on the Street
can cacophony

$
$$

$
$$

$$
$

$$
$

Game on

wantithaveitfigureitout
firsttoknowfirsttoget
firsttoshowmefirst

players all
raw energy
unapologetic

$
$$

$
$$

At the Exchange
commotion in motion
like roses trading thorns

$$ $$
$ $

Equity Justice
left the room

Are you staying?

On the side of
devil?
angel?

Under which star
is anyone
born?

$ 50 $
$$ $$

Bull Bear Dragon feed
fire
in their bellies
but
stay hungry

The Pit is not
on the Floor

Eating dinner tonight?

```
         BULLS
         E
         DRAGONS
HOPE     R
    S    SIZZLE
    I
    DREAM
    E
```

When Bull runs
everyone pants

when Bear guards
few game in

when Dragon fires
all get blazed

Mystagogue of
Bull Bear Dragon
instilled in
mystique of
humans?

Wizards
incognito all

belief in own
lies

Whose name
Merlin?

$$
$

$$
$

The swoon of power
paradise
you can't remember

Falling in love
or
falling apart?

$
$$

$
$$

Bulls Bears Dragons
huff down dry wells
listening for
answers?

$$ $$
$ $

Enough is enough

       bet you don't

       believe it enough

       stories are not

            Once   upon a time

$ $
$$ $$

Bull Bear Dragon
not restful creatures

lie between
heart and money

Wall Street wakens
their dreams of homestead

Pause

   let stillness reign
  silently turn round

       feel your heart
      catch your breath
     watch dust settle

          trepidation abates
             one moment
              might be

  significant

READ THE WALL

The power within
is
Dragon's breath
h e l d

Epilog

Morality in
our game of
win-lose?

TAILS UP!

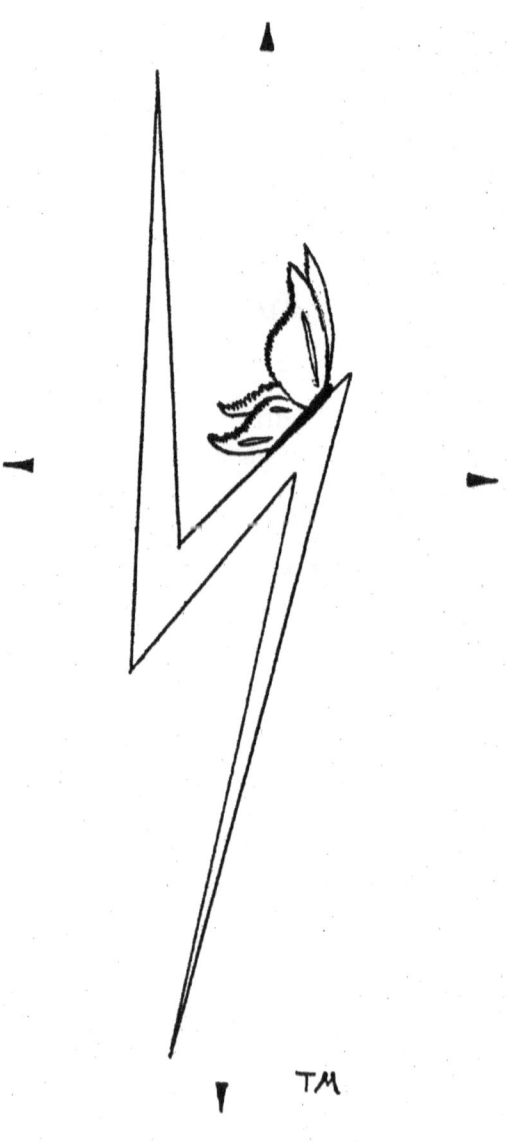

PhantasmaPress

www.ingramcontent.com/pod-product-compliance
Lightning Source LLC
Chambersburg PA
CBHW031545210526
45464CB00003B/1165